From the Inside Out:
Sonnets

by Brian Daldorph

From the Inside Out: Sonnets
Copyright 2008 by Brian Daldorph
International Standard Book Numbers
0-939391-48-1
978-0-939391-48-6

Manufactured in the United States of America
Woodley Press
Washburn University
Topeka, Kansas 66621
All Rights Reserved

First Edition

Cover Photo: Matt Porubsky
Author Photo: Brenna Daldorph
Cover Design: Christine Ewing
Book Design: Christine Ewing
Thanks to Pam LeRow, CLA&S Digital Media Services

For Thomas Zvi Wilson and Phil Miller.
And for Brenna and Lucy.

1.   Something like love

2.   Drink

6. Down Lonesome Road

7. Jail

I first discovered Brian Daldorph's poetry a few years ago in Lawrence, Kansas. The book was *The Holocaust and Hiroshima: Poems*, and I was fascinated with his use of "voice" in the poems, how the horrors and seriousness of World War II could be captured through persona. It was an example of how narrative poetry can go past history, past narrative, and that "place" can be found via persona and the lyric. When I think of the lyrical approach in poetry, it is through the "music" each line can make and how the "I" in each poem becomes blurred—how the "I" transcends into an "all-I". I think about Brian's persona poems in the way Li-Young Lee describes lyrical poetry: "There is a manifold of space and a manifold of time, a manifold consciousness." Brian's work is made out of this consciousness—where a poem is an act of compassion.

I am happy to be the editor for this collection, to introduce these sonnets, this time about Americans and their relationships. The sonnet form has a tradition of being about relationships, something overlooked when sonnets are defined as "a lyric poem of fourteen lines with a set rhyme scheme." The other quality about sonnets that is often forgotten is how each sonnet should have a *volta*—a turn—where a shift occurs. The shift is usually for a resolution to the "problem," but with poetry positioned in today's postmodern arena, the *volta* can be anything: tone, style, voice, etc.

This is what I enjoy about these poems: Brian keeps this tradition of sonnets while incorporating fresh voices—his voices of persona. His sonnets have a variety of slant rhyme schemes, if no rhyme at all, and the *volta* is not forced into the eighth line. Luckily, the ten-syllable-per-line rule is also not forced. This kind of play and innovation makes reading a pleasure. Maybe the room the sonnet form makes allows Brian to have the room for each person to tell her or his story, allowing a narrative to unfold in its lyrical approach.

These personas show the humor, anxiety, and heartbreak of America. In the opening poem "Math," the driving metaphor of the title turns into a mantra: "It doesn't add up." The "he" of the poem, in trying to figure out his relationship, becomes obsessed at solving a problem: "He's tried it this way, that. / Sometimes he doesn't sleep, he calculates all night." The *volta* of the poem occurs where it traditionally should, but is subtle within a sentence: "She kisses him outside his house / and then she's gone and not answering the phone." As the lover turns away, the turn occurs in the poem.

Brian's innovations in his sonnets are similar to what Gerald Stern did with his approach to the sonnet in his book *American Sonnets*. Stern did not set a line limit on his work, did not worry about rhyme schemes, and did not worry about line lengths either. However, Stern's work reads as autobiography, whereas Brian writes by borrowing different voices, to allow many points of view from the American psychic landscape. Lucky for us, we get to read about the effect American culture and position has for each persona, these lyrical narratives about Dodge Darts, a man who likes to dress like Scarlett O'Hara, Robert Johnson's talk with Satan, blue-collar workers, and even writers. Two of my favorite lines break the stereotype of someone in jail, how the person in jail cries "so nobody can hear him, keeps it hidden / like snapshots of his kids pinned up in his brain."

These poems are like Blues songs. The reader gets to feel the different landscapes of America, created in the different sections of this book, through the body—through lament. "the american dream" is here, too. *From the Inside Out* is an appropriate title, as we meet the "people" in these poems, hear their spoken and internal voices, and celebrate how Brian's poems express this manifold moment in America.

Dennis Etzel Jr.
April 2008

Poems from this collection have appeared or will appear in the following publications:

About a Girl, Surge: *Seam*
Bind: *Paper Street*
The Blue River, The Pink Dress, Prodigal Summer: *Envoi*
Cold Snap: *Tears in the Fence*
Dodge Dart: *Borderlines*
Fire: *Pennine Platform*
How to Love, 1205th Dream: *Pulsar*
Last Sonnet: *Lawrence Journal World*
Math, What I Saw From Where I Stood: *Kansas City Star*
Nowheresville: *North American Review*
One More Silver Dollar: *The Journal*
Out, Scrapper: *Poetry Scotland*
Penance: *Inscape*
A Quiet Drunk: *Smiths Knoll*
The Retired Fireman: *South*
Tea at the House: *Thorny Locust*
Straight, The Trial: *The Same*
Winter: *Rockhurst Review*

1. SOMETHING LIKE LOVE

MATH

It doesn't add up. He's tried it
every which way and still it comes up short:
the way she's always late and brings him another excuse,
like she had to wait for the repairman. Or she received bad news
but nothing she can talk about just now.
Then when he asks her to stay the night there's always
some reason she can't do it. "I'd love to," she says,
"but you know how it goes." She kisses him outside his house
and then she's gone and not answering the phone.
He figures it's easier to be alone than half-alone.
But some nights she'll come over and slip into his bed
and next morning tell him everything like she's emptying out her head.
It doesn't add up. He's tried it this way, that.
Sometimes he doesn't sleep, he calculates all night.

The long black car that burned money
pulling up outside our house. Then nothing,
and again nothing, until at last a door opening
slowly, slowly, then all the way.
You emerging, feet first, then your thighs then
your tight black dress like a dark river.
You're laughing and I hear, "Well, I never—"
and you're standing, brushing back your hair. Done.
You close the door and the car slides off.
You seem to be taking a deep breath of night air.
I'm watching and waiting for you to sneak in like a mouse.
You're hoping I'm asleep. You're making up lies, just in case.
I had dinner ready for you hours ago. You'll say,
"What else could I do? He was nice. We need the money."

DODGE DART

Bought it for fifty bucks and two jugs
of homemade wine. Sawdust
in the gearbox, and it drank oil
like my Dad swilled beer. Sure, it had bugs
in the carseats and sounded like Apollo 13 if I just
stepped on the gas. But I could pick up my girl
in her party dress and drive her to Ollie's house
where all the parties were that last summer
before Ollie got locked up and the rest of us
didn't hang out anymore. Then I stayed home for
weeks at a time until I found a job and tried
to stay afloat on Black Lake.
But that summer I drove my Dodge down First and Oak
with Lizzie beside me, pretty red hair in braids.

What is this place anyway? she asks. *It's a dump.*
The sort of place where junkies jump
out the window with the screaming heebie-jeebies.
How much do they want for this? Tell me it's a freebie.
I mean, what jerk would <u>pay</u> for this?
What I'd really like to do is kiss her
and say, *I know it's not much but it's all ours*
and we can each work three jobs and save up for a house
in a few years' time. Until then we'll be together.
But I know she won't let me hold her.
The John's broken and it stinks
like the shithouse in Hell. Roaches everywhere. I need a drink.
She's off and down the cracked front path.
I want to say, *We can do this!* But she's going fast.

1205TH DREAM

You again in my frontyard at night.
I'm sleeping but I know you're here, unloading
another truck. You're struggling up the front path like
Ms. Fed Ex with another load of gifts for me, bright
packages stacked on my front porch. "I don't want anything,"
I'd told you, but you'd not heard what I said.
I can't open my door. There's already a wall
of gifts and another truck pulling up, brakes
creaking, the driver cursing, grumbling, "I need to sleep."
You march from the truck with your arms full,
balancing one box on your head. "For heaven's sake,
what is all this?" I say when you wake me up,
so happy to be bringing me all your love.
Another truck arriving. All of Fed-Ex on the move.

PINK DRESS

Anything could happen when you wore that pink dress.
Our dentist said he'd divorce his wife
if you'd only give him hope. And when you went to confess
your sins, Father Connelly said he'd had enough of celibate life . . .
Let's just say that it opened steel doors.
That it made men act like whores.
That you turned the heads of statues, and men
lost for years found themselves again.
There was that guy in the airport who claimed
he was a millionaire and would give it all to you.
And that corporate lawyer who said he dreamed
that he'd back-pack with you in Kathmandu.
You couldn't stop what we called *Pink Dress Scenes.*
And then there was what happened when you wore cut-off jeans.

FEMININE SIDE

Sometimes it needed to assert
itself, you know? He'd slide into his wife's skirt
and blouse, then slip them off and try her dress.
And make-up! What a joy that was, the kiss
of lipstick on his dry lips, mascara
and all the little phials and pots of perfumes,
nail polish and foundation creams.
He liked dressing up as Scarlett O'Hara!
When his wife said, *I'm going out with the girls tonight,*
his heart leapt as though he had a lover!
But it was even better than that.
He had his whole feminine side to uncover or cover
in his wife's pretty clothes. Her strange look
when she'd walk in late, *Why so happy, Jack?*

THE TRIAL

It takes place in the basement
of my house. The judge sits
in my favorite armchair, wigged head bent
over pages of my sins. *Punishment must fit
the crime,* he tells the jury of my ex- friends
who nod in unison like engine parts.
Of course I know already how all this ends.
It's no secret that the judge hates my guts.
I stand and say, *I shall defend myself!*
But they're not telling me what I've done.
At night in my cell, alone,
I wish they'd let me be a traitor, murderer or thief.
The trial drags on. Tomorrow my ex-wife
will testify all about my sinful little life.

ANCIENT MARBLE WALLS

He gave her a coffee-table travel book
when she kept saying, "You never take me any place."
Not that they have a coffee table. But she'd stay up late
to read when he went to bed. (He had to get up early for work).
His idea of a good time was a road trip to Wichita,
dinner at a steak house then hit the bars.
Sometimes she'd bring her book along
and try to show him photographs of Dakar or Hong Kong
or any place that wasn't where they were.
He didn't see what all the fuss was about.
A lake was a goddamn lake, here or there.
He asked her if she'd like to smoke another cigarette.
What was it she wanted that she couldn't get from malls?
Something *foreign*. Cracked statues. Pink shells. Ancient marble walls.

Then I got older. It wasn't my fault
though Chuck seemed to think it was. Not
that he'd say that. But he'd be out of the house
every chance he got. He'd say, "I have to work late, Jess.
You know I have that book to get out." I knew.
But didn't know why he'd have to go to some bar
with his grad students for a drink or two.
"It's part of my job as a professor,"
he'd say in his best, sincere-sounding voice.
Those boy's blue eyes where not even weapons inspectors
could find anything bad. He's just good old Chuck Taylor
who loves his kids and *MASH* and hot sauce.
There must be some pretty girl with green eyes and red hair
who loves him the way I first did, with fire, with fire.

ABOUT A GIRL

He can't stop thinking about kissing her.
She doesn't think of him at all.
Or when she does it's because he's quietly harassing her,
sitting next to her at lunch, *Hi, what's the deal?*
When she wheels herself back to her room
he steers his frame down the hall:
it's one o'clock, time
for exercise, *Get Fit, Stay Well.*
Later he writes her a letter,
slips it in a blue envelope.
If he doesn't keep trying she'll find someone better
like Arthur, or Matthew, or damn Percy Knapp
with his silly moustache and Southern charm.
He'd like to whack him with his walker, bust his arm.

you told me was to quit my damn job:
"It's killing you," you said, like you knew.
"Look at me," you said. "No one owns me, I do
whatever I want to do. You'd best take a stab
at freedom before it all dries up and blows away."
When I said it might take a week to wind things up
at the office, you yelled, "Start today!
If you don't do it now then you'll never stop
working like a lackey for crappy pay.
The Revolution starts here!" "Damn right,"
I said. "I'll call my boss and say 'I quit.'
What do you think of *that*?"
You kissed me then, said, "Let's stay in bed all day
and watch movies, what do you say?"
I tried to sound excited. "ok. ok. OK. OK!"

BREAK UP

I'm leaving you, his wife says,
and what's he supposed to do, break down, beg her to stay?
He folds up his newspaper, *OK.*
He supposes there are some arrangements to be made.
First night she's gone he's good to himself:
half bottle of wine and that joint he'd saved
in a tobacco tin back of a book shelf.
He guesses she just ran out of love,
which happens. Happened to his brother-in-law
who ran off with a schoolgirl, leaving his sister
to raise three kids. Would he miss her,
his wife? Sometimes she could be an awful bore.
Then there was Alice at work, and Stacey
just broken up with her husband, saying, *Call me, call me.*

It's never the right time.
Why should I spoil our night out
at a Thai restaurant when your face is full of light
and you say, *Everything rhymes!*
I could say, *I have something to tell you,*
and you'd open up those blue, blue
eyes, and I'd say, *Oh, it's nothing at all,*
and fiddle with my ring, lock up my soul.
If you love me you'd say, *Whatever you tell me,*
nothing will change. But what words can I find
to say something that's burning up my mind?
You look so happy!
Later I try to sleep with rats in my heart
and your arms around me all night.

BIND

That book he'd read in school, *Knots,*
written by some shrink whose job it was to untie
them. How she felt hurt by him and he felt hurt
because she felt hurt and on and on, tight
in a bind like seals caught in fishing twine.
He was angry with her for what she'd done and not done
and she felt she'd acted in her own best interest
and was up in arms about his unfairness,
how he'd tried to make it all her fault.
Now he wouldn't back down and lose face,
and she certainly wasn't shifting. Dead halt.
They'd be stuck for life. Nothing to save.
They were trapped and there was no way to break
out. And only their lives at stake.

As though we are *civilized.*
As though we'd never spat in each other's eyes.
As though I'd not said, "May you burn in Hell!"
"Milk? Sugar?" You play the part so well.
And the conversation? About this and that:
the leaky roof, our daughter's field trip, the sick cat.
We've locked up all we really need to say
about ruined lives and treachery.
Your new woman, our ex-nanny, is polite.
She brings in cakes she's made and you make a joke
about keeping the kitchen tidy: *I never did that.*
So many broken things. So many that don't work.
But this does, for a little while, this sipping tea
and stirring sugar into pretty cups of misery.

PRODIGAL SUMMER

That was the summer when you longed
for girls until your whole body hurt.
You'd steal your friend's *Playboys*. You did not belong
in that world of perfect flesh and wet mouths, but
you had to force your way in, under the covers,
imagining what it would be like with your friend's sister, say.
She had her own pretty boy lovers.
You watched her with them and honestly
they might as well have been on Mars.
The scent of flowers clogged your throat.
The sun burnt you. You could not sleep at night
with all those girls around. You walked for hours.
You knew this different, wretched kind of sad.
It was the prodigal summer you never had.

STRONG MEDICINE

The only thing
we agreed on was that something was wrong.
That, and that we didn't do things by halves.
You said you knew what would cure us,
that it would cut us up like knives.
It sounded so *good,* so much better than booze.
You poured the strong medicine into paper cups:
it burnt straight through them, cut
the tablecloth to shreds. I liked the look of this.
We poured what was left into glass
bowls, then raised them like chalices.
Strong medicine smoked and fizzed and sparked;
we tipped it back like we were diving into dark.
Joy of it! As though fire
coursing through us would purge and cure.

OUT

Helen said, *Jeff, I love you, but not like that,*
and he said, *Fine,*
we can still be friends, if that's what
you'd like. She said, *Jeff, you'll make some woman*
very happy. He was thinking,
Stop messing me around.
They were driving back into town
from visiting his mother who'd been beaming
on them all the time in her kitchen.
When Helen went out for a walk,
Jeff's mother said, *She's lovely, don't let this one go,*
as though he'd just gotten a new dog or new truck.
He'd said, *We're taking it slow.*
But he was driving fast back into town.
He'd drop her off, buy a bottle and drown.

COLD SNAP

She says she has this vision of the two of us
in a book-lined room: "I'll rise
to put a book back, stop behind you and caress
your shoulders with my hands." She kisses
the back of my neck. I don't look up.
Cold snap
in the warm room, seventeen degree
drop. "Are you trying to ignore me?"
"Sorry, I was reading my book,
Journey Around My Bedroom. My head was stuck
in it. I didn't mean to be rude."
But her face is flushed. She's mad
at me for being distant, cold.
And this is how we shall grow old.

2. DRINK

There was only one time when I slipped up.
I'd played tough.
I'd said, *Never again. Not one more drop.*
It was easy enough
at first. I went along to meetings, said my stuff
about how it had gotten to the point where I could not stop:
beer for breakfast, liquid lunch then a bottle
for afternoon in the park. Those guys knew the score.
Stretched tight afternoons at home with a kettle
and seventeen cups of coffee until my head was caffeine sore.
But I was doing it, one day, then the next and on and on.
Then there was a bottle in my hand again.
I snapped off the top, took the first big hit
and it was glorious. And. I. Was. In. Deep. Shit.

AMBITION

"A drunk," I'd said, when I was asked who I'd be
in twenty years. I knew me,
knew I'd be half-happy with a dirty flat
in some city, near the bars, near the jazz,
where nobody would tell me to get a job.
Now if I have money I drink it, and my daughters
sometimes find me, feed me, clean up, tell me to stop
wasting my life. But they're gone faster
than my last one-night stand.
I tell them I have it all planned:
a few years of this then I'll straighten out.
I have a bottle in for the night.
What had I known about what booze destroys?
I'd thought it was kind of cool, a smart choice.

DENIAL

Some days she'll deny herself tea.
We're not talking large-scale suffering here
but a small dose of misery
to make pleasures sharper, clearer.
The way she gave up alcohol like the Mayor
of Casterbridge who stopped stone cold.
It hurt a bit, sure,
but here's what's odd: she got
more drunk on denial than she ever was
on booze! Then there were cigarettes.
No games with that:
she quit and stayed quit.
And sort of wished she had another addiction to fix.
Food? Love? She could do it.

THE DRUNKARD'S WIFE

This time he's calling from Maidstone,
in a prison cell,
Can I come right away with bail?
Paul, my alcoholic man,
I didn't cause it, can't control
or cure it, just have to deal
with it all over again. He wants me
to drive to Maidstone in the rain
and drive home with Paul vowing
never again, *never* again, I'll have his word
on that, his word—but what's that worth?
Do I turn out tonight, winter blowing
into my head, car windows down?
Or do I stay home alone?

A QUIET DRUNK

This he's good at, *this* he can believe
unlike all that junk about love,
how that's all he'll ever need.
So when his latest lover tells him
she's *so* sorry but she has to quit,
he's cool, thanks her for what they've had.
He knows exactly what to do:
bottle of Smirnoff,
ice in the refrigerator and the night off,
Marlboro and Robert Johnson blues.
Sometimes he calls her late,
mutters even more thanks and she says, "Great,
that's great but I can't talk now."
Fine, he doesn't need her anyhow.

3. THEM BLUES

PRODIGAL WINTER

Winter she likes best:
it's shorter
on expectations, the plain daughter
who doesn't have to do best
at everything, who can settle
for a warm, dry room,
notebooks, a few hours at home
with box of Sleepytime tea and reliable kettle.
She doesn't have to slog out in sleet
to interact with nature as though that
has some worth. Nature is dead
and she watches it through her frozen window, bled
white as snow and cold as her white paper.
She can take it any way she wants. Nothing to stop her.

SCRAPPER

Hemingway told me how to do it:
Write one true sentence and then one more,
one more. And the thing is that you must actually do it,
no matter what it takes, speed, whiskey, a whore
for later when you need to break away.
Sure there's some madness in it, sure.
What did you expect? Tranquility? A day
in the office then drive home in your new car?
No, no, it's always the same wherever you are,
in Paris, Tunis, Athens, or Zanzibar,
it's you and the page, slugging it out
until you rise, punch-drunk, and you've won the bout.
Sometimes when it's going well it can be goddamn fun.
But you'll end up staring into the dark eye of a gun.

THEM BLUES

Robert Johnson crawled out of his grave
like it was the morning after
a big drunk. That he didn't know where he was
was nothing new. That he didn't know who was with him
was nothing new too. Just then the door opened.
"What ya doin' here so early, Satan?"
The man in the black suit with Cuban cigar
stinking up the room stepped in.
"I got three more songs for you, Mr. Johnson,
and I'll be takin' the next installment on your soul."
It was a good deal, Robert thought.
I mean, who needs a soul anyways?
Not when you can moan them Crossroads Blues,
and play guitar like there's a lightning storm inside.
Not when you can catch that Greyhound bus to hell and ride.

LAST SONNET

He needed to write.
He'd sit at the kitchen table late night
and his wife would say, *I'm turning in,*
and he'd not stop writing or look up, *Fine.*
You do that. I'll join you soon.
He knew she wished he'd come to her
but she left him to his "Melancholy Blues," that old jazz tune
they'd listened to so often that first summer.
She was always asleep by the time he came to bed.
Sometimes she wished she could look inside his head
to see what was happening there that he would not show.
Poems, yes, occasionally. But no
poem was worth the way he had of being off limits to her.
The way he'd sit in the kitchen with razor wire perimeter.

She doesn't turn to me. *I have,*
she says, as though talking to a child, *poems to write.*
I shouldn't have to tell you. She has her knife
out, so I say, *Of course not. I'll go shave.*
I leave her to her fierce craft,
scrunched over the page like she has to force her heart
out through the thin black tube in her hand.
I turn on the TV, watch this movie I don't understand,
all cut-up images and some foreign gibberish.
I'd be happier watching, *You Wanna Be Rich?*
She'd gotten a poem published in some podunk magazine
and now she thinks she's Emily Dickinson.
Who was it said he'd have all writers shot?
Me, after too many beers and cigarettes.

LAST WORD

God knows the number of words I'll write.
God knows my first word
and He's been keeping score since then,
even when I'm up past midnight
listening to night trains and Yardbird,
trying to hold onto my heavy black pen.
Sometimes I think I could write forever,
just sit at my desk and not move
beyond the twitching of my hand. I'd not need a lover.
Words would be my picture-framed love.
Eventually there'd be only my last word left
to write. Perhaps I'd think about it for days,
stretched out on my death bed.
What should it be? *Rain? Sea? Alone? Amaze?*

WINTER

By the tropical birdhouse, shut down
for winter, she sits
with Starbucks coffee and cigarettes.
She loves the swirling patterns
of her breath in the air.
She was another woman here,
laughing at the crazy things he'd said,
insisting that he'd still love her
if she weighed three-fifty, addicted
to chocolate and cheese snacks.
Winter tugs at her hair.
What a cold joke,
all he'd said, all they'd planned,
dead leaves scuttling across the ground.

AFTER LIFE

I don't want to hear about my son.
All I need to know is that he's not joined
me here. No doubt he's doing fine.
My daughter? She was always one to take command
and get exactly what she wanted.
She said I'd watch over her, but she's not haunted.
I know my dog was well cared for until she died.
I cried for her, I cried.
My house? Knock it down.
It was just where I stayed when
there was no other place to go. No one
could say I didn't care. It's just that cares were no longer mine
by the time I'd used up all the years I had to live.
But tell me, damn you, did my poems survive?

4. LORD, PLEASE LET ME OUT OF HERE

How is he planning to do it?
It will be his last job.
He'll work on it in his workshop
on winter days with a small heater.
He'll do fine work, of course.
He'll go off to the lumber yard for wood.
Pine or birch. He'll paint it with creosote.
He'll lie down beside it to test it for size.
I mean, why waste money on a fancy one
when he can make one himself just as good?
With his trusty tools, his chisel, plane,
hammer, saw. The lid fitting neatly, of course.
And the only thing that won't be done
is to screw that coffin lid down.

When Frank got laid off at the plastics factory
he couldn't tell his wife, Annette.
She'd been reading about lay-offs in *The Mercury*,
and when she asked, Frank said, "They're not cutting me yet."
He'd still get up at 5 a.m., make coffee, pack a lunch,
start up his truck then kiss Annette goodbye.
Losing your job is like a big slow punch.
He'd drive by the factory gates at first light.
Nothing to do all day but drive around,
or park his truck at some gas stop and sit
drinking coffee, reading sports, eating donuts,
trying not to think about what was happening to his town.
He'd walk by the river and wonder where it led,
and if he toppled in, where they'd find him, dead.

I made up my bed with clean sheets.
I didn't think I could do so much.
I'd checked in here so I could simply sit
in a corner and stare like a man punched
into submission. I submitted.
But I had a room-mate, Leroy, who pretended
to be asleep but hopped up as soon as the door closed.
"What you score, man? What you score?" He was after my dose
of blues and oranges and greens. "Straight or bent?"
he asked. "I didn't come here to talk.
I came here to get my mind back."
Dr. Murphy said he'd be round at eight to tuck me in.
"If there's anything you want then just hang on
to your dick and pray," he said. He thought I was a fake.
I heard him tell his nurse, "Just another flake."

I hate the way she rattles on about
what she did when she was a little girl. I hate
the way she digs into drawers that stink
of mildew and dust because she thinks
I'll be interested in some ancient brown and white
photographs of ghost-faced people whose names she can't quite
remember: "That might be cousin Alexander or my friend
Marianne. My memory's not what it was, I'm afraid."
All I want to do is watch *The Deep End*
on Channel 10. I pray my mother will come soon. Pray and pray.
Grandma shows me the ring that Grandpa gave her
a hundred or a thousand years ago, she can't quite remember
and big deal, it's a stone stuck in gold.
I wish she'd shut up. Or do the next thing after being old.

EDINBURGH

It's never as bright as *the blues.*
For her it's always grey,
grey light in her window when she wakes.
Same old dreary radio news
while she pours grey
milk into her *Weetabix* bowl.
That song by Nick Drake:
grey grey grey grey grey moon.
Drizzle as she hurries to the train station.
No streetlamps, just cold rain
down her neck, slithering
down her back. Why fight it,
the Grey Disease? Why go looking
for color? Why get out of grey sheets?

LAST POEM

He thinks of Whitman spending his last strength
on his beloved, *Leaves of Grass.*
If only his one life stretched out for an unending length
of months, days, weeks and years! Instead, loss,
and the one book he'd leave behind,
the beautiful wild offspring of the poet's mind.
Now there's only time for this one last
poem: how to sum up all his life
with sand slipping through his fingers fast.
It must include, he reckons, his wives, his children, this house,
what it felt like in spring to loaf by the river
and all the stories he'd heard and told about lovers.
What word for the gathering fall?
Everything. Nothing. Nothing at all.

HOMECOMING

He had some needles and bags of junk.
His mother said, "Oh, David, how thin you are!"
and smelt liquor on his breath, and knew he was drunk
and it was only half past four.
David said, "It's so good to be home," the way he always did,
kissed her then hauled his stuff up to his room.
To make it through the day he'd need a hit.
He felt that odd tingling in his arm.
He thought his mother wouldn't know
when he went downstairs high,
as though she couldn't see that glow,
as though she didn't know that he would die and she would die.
"I've made your favorite, chicken salad and fresh bread."
As though she could keep him alive with her food.

One little white pill a day was what the doctor said
would cure me. One little white pill was no good.
I read the instructions: *Take once a day with food.*
But what was I supposed to do all that night, all next day
until it was pill time again?
Stare out the window and count the white birds?
I'd been sick long enough. I wanted to be cured.
I popped one pill, then another. I took ten.
And stopped. Best not to take too much strong medicine.
When my blood started to boil,
I was cool:
I sat in a bathtub full of ice.
If it didn't hurt like hell what good could it do?
I'd get better if it killed me. I started turning blue.

PLEASANT VALLEY

Who can I tell my stories to?
The nice nurses finish their shifts and go--
Anna, Marie, Minnie, Flo.
My brother's still alive, last I heard,
but we haven't talked since February twenty-third
nineteen ninety three when he told me
I'd gotten bald and fat,
and I said, "Henry, Screw You!"
I'd always wanted to say that.
My daughter died in a car crash.
My wife died at forty-four.
Most days I just stare
out the window and repeat my prayer:
Lord, please let me out of here.

5. FIRE

FIRE

As a boy I loved it, the flare of matches,
spurt of fire. I'd stare at candles
until they burnt down, watching smoke
twist up toward the sky, as though I'd been snatched
by some fire god whose hands
were gentle flames. I'd chase after fire trucks
in the street and pray
I could watch flames rage through a house,
a drunken god stumbling round his home.
Cold nights were best. My chilly back and hot face,
and those plumes of water like slow flashes
and firemen yelling and hurling themselves into flame.
I did not dream of girls, I dreamt of fire,
that welling lava of desire.

THE FIREMAN

He has to keep a fire burning in his house
at all times. In the bedroom closet, maybe,
or in the basement behind the old couch.
And if his wife smells burning, he says, *It's nothing, baby.*
Even on the hottest days of summer, he
has to have fire. Lights it early
morning when his wife's still sleeping.
He just has to take what he needs and she
can't give. Flame. And even better, secret fire.
He strips off his clothes and dances
before it, as though he's bringing flowers to the altar
of his lover. Wild, wild he dances.
When his wife asks why he's fever hot,
the fireman wants to tell her, but cannot.

Any fireman worth his burns will tell you, *You never
know when or how a fire might start.*
Some careless kid with a firecracker,
short-circuiting, a hot saucepan, car exhaust.
I've seen an apartment block burn because of a spark
from a hair drier. I've pulled bodies out of ash
because some joker thought he'd smoke in the dark,
tossed a lit cigarette in the trash.
I keep having this dream of a house in flames
and I'm standing watching but can't do a thing.
There are children screaming, my wife's yelling,
Fireman, fireman, save us, save our homes!
I throw myself upon her, smother the flame,
my tears falling, falling, hot rain.

FIRE AGAIN

He'd pulled kids out of burning houses, sure,
smashing his way into flame like the Viet Cong.
Sometimes it felt like his hose was an M-16.
Some reporter asked him why he'd chosen to fight fire
and he felt like he'd been asked to sing his favorite song
and couldn't remember the first word. "What was that again?"
So much sitting around or taking walks
with his firemen buddies round a couple of blocks.
Women on the force now which he doesn't like
because some things a woman can't do under fire
but he keeps his mouth shut or he'll lose his job.
He'd go crazy trying to sell cars on some Crooked Jack lot.
That thrill in his blood when there's fire again
burning inside him, that pure flame.

THE RETIRED FIREMAN

still longs for blazing flame,
for arriving *at the scene,* sirens screaming—
he's never had a woman who's given him more.
First he has to smash down the door.
He can still feel the power of an axe in his hand.
Sometimes he'll pick up a fire call on his Emergency Band
radio and drive out to feel again that surge
of adrenaline, that wildness trying to get out, that urge
to battle flame at any cost.
He wishes he were not lost
in the world of safety pins and coffee cups
and one more Fall, one more furnace to start up.
He needs fire, and what he hadn't realized
is how it gets into your blood, your soul, your eyes.

6. DOWN LONESOME ROAD

Never mind. I start making a lemon meringue pie.
Never mind. He was like all the others, he stayed
long enough to make me cry
when he left with the Chardonnay and loaf of French bread.
He'd talked about his work in City Hall,
how he was the man who kept the city turning over
because if traffic tickets weren't processed we'd be in Hell.
He kept saying that bald, fat men make the best lovers.
I had a stash of food for when he left.
I knew I'd have to treat myself to cheese and chocolate,
biscuits and butter cake. I'll stay up late.
Tomorrow clear up another mess.
Never mind, if I have to I'll live alone my whole damn life.
I'll not be gutted by some man with a little knife.

ON THE ROAD

Two days later and it's Spring Falls,
South Dakota, and this part-time job at the Conoco
pumping gas for shoppers at the Great Mall.
He could pick up a waitress called Maggie or Jo.
Or take a bottle back to his roach motel
and watch some ball game from another world.
Sometimes he wonders if this is some prison cell,
that he doesn't even notice he's in jail.
He'll give it two months here then quit
and drive on to Reno or Cedar City
or some place else with a job and a bar and a diner
where he can chat with women with tattoos and eyeliner.
Maybe you're only loved by one woman or two
in your whole life. When they're gone, where do you go?

ANGEL

You can't figure out who paid her to come:
it wasn't a friend because you don't have friends.
Your brothers died in the war or at home
with holes in their arms. Your sister sends
letters telling you where you can find Christ.
But there's this woman at your door in a red dress
and silly party hat with big smile
like she knows exactly what's best.
You'd like her smile if she had nice eyes.
But she's got black holes and her mouth's
a large dry cave where bats and flies
disturb the dark. She knows the truth
about love and death, God and sin.
She'll tell you everything if you only let her in.

BY THE SEA

She sits alone and stares out
at the sea, the sea, and wishes for
the sea's patience, its way of never
accepting the small defeat
of each wave expending itself on the beach
then trickling back. She should do this.
She's hungry and needs to piss.
She must be alive, she has appetites, needs.
It was never going to be like this, a lonely
old woman living in a seaside flat
with daffodils in a vase, two fat cats
and another Sainsbury's cake and pot of tea.
The next day, the next, on and on,
and by the kitchen table, her cold telephone.

RAMBLER

Some mornings he wakes and can't remember where
and he needs to reach out and touch his guitar
beside him like a woman should be.
Ohio, Kansas, Des Moines, Rockport, Tennessee:
always some place he's going, something out there
beyond the next song scribbled in the parking lot
watching the funeral procession of trucks and cars,
beyond the next cup of coffee and cigarette.
Sometimes he finds some cheap motel,
buys a six-pack and pizza, watches TV
and falls asleep, wakes to the TV's yell.
Always some other place to drive to, free.
He's King of America, he can go anywhere.
Except to Springfield. To Anna's eyes, her hair.

BLUE JAZZ

It's one too many cans of soup
and French bread from Food Star bakery.
It's one too many bottles of 7-Up
and apple slices, Earl Grey tea
with a good book or with some bebop CD,
as though Charlie Parker, Coltrane or Dizzy
could pump out of him those blue blue blues.
This was just meant to be what he did to get him through
that first summer he'd be alone
after she packed up her truck and moved out to Oregon.
He'd wait, he'd always waited, and she'd come back
with sob stories, lies, fingertips on his neck.
Perhaps he should call his mother.
One more night of bread, soup, jazz. Then another.

HOW TO LOVE

It's easy enough, really. First,
you have to get broken. I mean, really smashed up
inside. Be Lear on the heath, cursing at the storm, *Worst!*
Do your worst! Tear out my gray hair! Don't stop
until I'm beaten into dirt! Got it?
Next, spend a few seasons in the woods
nursing your wounds with a paste of millet
seeds, nettles, and bay leaves. Food?
Berries, birds' eggs and honeysuckle.
When you start thinking that this is your lot
then you're almost there. Hunger? Sure. Buckle
down to it. Some pretty maiden lost in the woods? Of course not.
Your skinny fingers like a dead man's bones.
Then you realize, you *love* to be alone.

SURGE

She endures day in the sickly light
of her office where she works
for nothing but a paycheck
and that time she clocks out.
Some nights she has to stop off at the liquor store
to buy a bottle of wine.
Sometimes she just has to get away from here
and booze is cheaper than a flight.
That *surge* of relief when she gets home
and night's all hers, curtains shut.
She did get up this morning, she's earned this
time alone in her own house
with John Coltrane pouring out his heart
and liquor loving her from the inside out.

HOME IS WHERE THE TEA IS

One of her selves stays home, the one
who likes tea and toast and *Time* magazine
more than anything, a little too much.
(Definitely more than a lover's touch).
She can take a bath at 11 a.m.
and then just sit in a white chair in her white home
and beam on all that's hers.
She could stay here years and years,
writing letters and reading all her favorite books
over and over again.
Maybe something happens to the brain
at a certain age and you don't have to plan
that next flight to Mexico or Rome.
One of you, at least, can stay home.

He stays that night outside Blue Falls,
sleeps in his car, a few hours at least
before a cop raps on his windshield. Breakfast
at a truck stop with sleek Country Western singers on the walls
and the jukebox filling up his head with songs
about cheatin' women and miles down Lonesome Road.
A dead-eyed waitress serves him coffee in Clear Springs.
He wonders if in death you have to pay back what you owe.
Millers Ford, Shawnee Heights, Monrovia, Chase City,
spends the night at a motel in Allen Town.
Sometimes he lies in bed and fiddles with the phone.
What would he hear in her voice? Anger? Relief? Pity?
She'd likely say, "Where the hell are you?"
He'd hang up because he wouldn't know.

CROSS

Her mother still called her James.
She'd never accept that a son of hers . . .
But Jamie would go home to her and say, *Mom, Mom, Mom,*
I never was a boy. I was a girl trapped, cursed
to be in the body of a boy then a man.
"God made you the way He intended you to be."
Then they'd both start crying. Why did everything add up to pain?
At least James had never brought home with him a "friend."
Is this how it would always end,
no one eating, no one talking, just heavy looks
and that son of hers, now a daughter, with her head in some book?
She had a daughter who would not visit when James was there,
a pretty girl, with three little children, golden-haired.

FATHER AND SON

Don't mistake me. I'm not advocating
my way as *the way,* the truth and light,
like my father did, that evil sod.
The way he saw it, anyone who didn't praise God
was doomed to everlasting night.
Beyond salvation. No happy awakening.
My mother would say, "Daddy's a little mad again,"
when he'd lock his bedroom door and rant,
preparing for his Sunday morning sermon,
the next installment of his treatise on sin and pain
and how every sinner could be turned into a saint.
I'd doodle on my church program. Listen to rain.
My father all in black like God's muscular goon.
And I was in the back row, his forsaken son.

PENANCE

I liked this part the most:
the way I could pay for my sins
with prayers I'd say in the chill
chapel, "Father, Son and Holy Ghost—"
I'd ask the priest behind the screen
for more. "That's hardly enough for what I've done,"
I'd say. I wanted to be on my knees all afternoon
to be absolutely sure I'd paid for my sins.
I was like a Red Guard waving my Red Book.
Like a recruit informing his Corporal
that he didn't want to be treated like a girl.
I wanted real bullets. I wanted glass in my socks.
There was no paying for sin without blood.
There was no small way to pay God what I owed.

THE POSSIBLE

Of course Denise might call, say, *How*
could I have been so <u>stupid</u>?
Do you think you can forgive me for what I did?
Then I'll be merciful, *You reap what you sow,*
I'll say, as though I know what I'm talking about.
Or that editor will call and say, *I read your book*
and I must have it. It's great. Let's meet
as soon as possible. Did I mention that I love your work?
Or my sister to say, *You're right and now I see it:*
it was all my fault. Or my teacher: *You were the best kid*
I ever taught. Or that woman who stood on Ninth Street
and talked and smiled, raking fingers through gorgeous hair.
If I wait a little longer, I'll hear from her.
She's coming my way. Wait. Wait just a little longer.

7. JAIL

OUTSIDE

He don't do drugs no more. Quit
after the fourth time he went to jail.
If you do drugs it don't take long till there's a cop's boot
on back of your neck, then you're in a jail cell.
He don't drink no more. He's drunk away
two wives, a few kids, houses, all his money
and ended up in some alley in a cardboard box.
Never did have a go at crack
though it was all around him on the street.
But he's got this apartment now, and hot
meals twice a day at Salvation Army
and this lady friend who comes round to watch TV.
Some nights when it hurts too much and he needs his fill
he loads up on three bottles of Nyquil.

IN THE JAILHOUSE NOW

He's always arrested in November, spends
a few months in County Jail
until March or April, the end
of Kansas winter. No one to post bail.
His best friends are these guys on the inside
who know how life can shit and shit
on you, know what it takes to survive:
some God to pray to,
those poems he writes
and can't stop writing, though likely they'll not see the light
of anyone else's eyes.
And when he's got to cry he learns to cry
so nobody can hear him, keeps it hidden
like snapshots of his kids pinned up in his brain.

FALL

He needs this cell. It was getting cold
out there and he'd done all the drugs he could buy.
It was either jail or die.
Sometimes he thinks he's getting too old
for this shit, but it's too late to start over
with some sweet-eyed lover
who says, "You and only you are the man I love."
He'd be late for his wedding again,
and what woman would choose a man with cracked brain?
He sees the young punks in here scared
about what they've gotten into, not
the cocky kids they were on the street who dared
to run faster than the cops. He ended up in this cell
where it's warm enough. And three hot meals.

STRAIGHT

For SP, back inside

Said you'd had enough of this shit.
Said you'd had enough of getting out
with all the good intentions in your head
and those good guys glad to see you
with their little gifts to clear away the jailhouse blues:
My friend, you need this so bad.
Said you'd be hanging out in libraries not bars.
Said you had this work to do finding out
what this crazy life's all about,
and that jailhouse teacher told you about these writers
you should check out and you tried.
But certain temptations cannot be denied.
You left library books in your girlfriend's car,
went to see Mr. Woo in the Top Hat Bar.

JAIL

He's not like the guys in here full
of excuses, like it wasn't really his fault
because someone told him what to pull:
drive that car across town, run a packet to Cool Joe,
sell a baggy to a rich kid on Diamond Street.
He did what he did, it was his gig.
He's not a victim of any system
but his own. He's done all the crimes
he was nailed for, and a few more as well.
He likes to sit in his cell and read,
play chess or Solitaire.
Though guys in here moan at night and cry,
"God, I wanna die, please let me die,"
this jailhouse ain't quite hell.

Brian Daldorph teaches at the University of Kansas and at Douglas County Jail. He has also taught in Japan, Zambia, Senegal and England. He is the author of three other full-length books of poems: *The Holocaust and Hiroshima: Poems*, *Outcasts* (both Mid-America P), and *Senegal Blues* (219 P). He edits *Coal City Review*.